About Birds

About Birds
A Guide for Children

Cathryn Sill

Illustrated by John Sill

PEACHTREE PUBLISHERS, LTD.
Atlanta

For the One who created birds.
Genesis 1:21

Published by
PEACHTREE PUBLISHERS, LTD.
494 Armour Circle, NE
Atlanta, GA 30324

Text © 1991 Cathryn Sill
Illustrations © 1991 John C. Sill

Design by Candace J. Magee

Manufactured in Mexico
Printed and bound by Impresora Donneco Internacional S.A. de C.V.
R.R. Donnelley & Sons Co., División Reynosa/McAllen

10 9 8 7 6 5 4 3 2 1

Library of Congress Cataloging in Publication Data

Sill, Cathryn P., 1953-
    About birds / written by Cathryn Sill ; illustrated by John Sill.
        p. cm.
    Summary: Text and illustrations introduce the world of birds from eggs
to flight, from songs to nests.
    ISBN 1-56145-028-6 : $14.95
    1. Birds--Juvenile literature. [1. Birds.] I. Sill, John, ill. II. Title./
QL676.2.S53 1991   91-16654
598--dc20   CIP
                                  AC

About Birds

Birds have feathers.

PLATE 1
Northern Cardinal

Baby birds hatch from eggs.

Some birds build nests on the ground.

PLATE 3
Ovenbird

John Gill

Some build in very high places.

PLATE 4
Bald Eagle

And some do not build a nest at all.

PLATE 5
Common Murre

Birds travel in different ways.

PLATE 6
Canada Geese

Most birds fly,

PLATE 7
Ruby-throated Hummingbird

but some swim,

PLATE 8
Wood Ducks

and others run.

PLATE 9
Greater Roadrunner

John Gill

Birds may flock together

or live alone.

PLATE 11
Great Horned Owl

Birds use their bills to gather food.

a.

b.

c.

d.

e.

They sing to let other birds know how they feel.

PLATE 13
Indigo Bunting

Birds come in all sizes.

Birds are important to us.

PLATE 15
Backyard

Afterword

PLATE 1.
Feathers protect birds from the elements. Because feathers are so light and strong, they enable birds to fly.

PLATE 2.
Although all birds hatch from eggs, different species have different nesting habits.

PLATE 3.
The ovenbird gets its name from its nest, a small dome-shaped structure resembling an old-fashioned oven.

PLATE 4.
Many birds build nests above the ground, varying the height according to the needs of individual species.

PLATE 5.
The common murr lays its pointed pear-shaped eggs right on rocky ledges. The elongated shape of the eggs causes them to roll in a circular motion, thus preventing them from toppling off the edge.

PLATE 6.
Canada Geese are strong flyers. They are able to migrate hundreds of miles in spring and fall.

PLATE 7.
Male ruby-throated hummingbirds beat their wings around 70 times per second. Hummingbirds are able to hover and even fly backwards.

PLATE 8.
The wood duck has webbed feet that enable it to swim. It is also a strong flyer.

PLATE 9.
The greater roadrunner has been clocked running at speeds up to 20 m.p.h. They are able to fly, but do so reluctantly.

PLATE 10.
Red-winged blackbirds flock in winter for protection. But, during the nesting season, each pair has its own territory.

PLATE 11.
Many birds of prey are solitary.

PLATE 12.
Birds also use their bills to preen their feathers, build nests and defend themselves.

PLATE 13.
Birds use their voices to attract mates, defend their territory and warn others of danger.

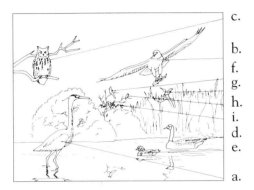

c.
b.
f.
g.
h.
i.
d.
e.

a.

PLATE 14.
The sizes of the illustrated birds are:
    a. Great blue heron—length 38", wingspread 70";
    b. Bald eagle—length 32", wingspread 80";
    c. Great horned owl—length 20",wingspread 55";
    d. Canada goose—length 16"-25", wingspread 50"-68";
    e. Wood duck—length 13 1/2", wingspread 28";
    f. Cardinal—length 7 3/4";
    g. Red-winged blackbird—length 7 1/4";
    h. Indigo bunting—length 4 1/2";
    i. Ruby-throated hummingbird—length 3 3/4"

PLATE 15.
Birds benefit people in many ways. They eat harmful insects, pollinate some flowers, disperse seeds, and keep rodent populations down. Observing birds brings great pleasure to many.

photo by Fred Eldredge

Elementary school teacher Cathryn Sill is an avid birder, as is her husband John, an award-winning and widely published wildlife artist. They live in Franklin, North Carolina, and are co-authors, with John's brother Ben Sill, of A FIELD GUIDE TO LITTLE-KNOWN & SELDOM-SEEN BIRDS OF NORTH AMERICA and ANOTHER FIELD GUIDE TO LITTLE-KNOWN & SELDOM-SEEN BIRDS OF NORTH AMERICA (Peachtree).